DISCOVER
BIG CATS

Titles in the *Discover Animals* series:

Discover Big Cats
ISBN-13: 978-0-7660-3473-0
ISBN-10: 0-7660-3473-9

Discover Bugs
ISBN-13: 978-0-7660-3472-3
ISBN-10: 0-7660-3472-0

Discover Sharks
ISBN-13: 978-0-7660-3474-7
ISBN-10: 0-7660-3474-7

Discover Snakes
ISBN-13: 978-0-7660-3471-6
ISBN-10: 0-7660-3471-2

DISCOVER ANIMALS

DISCOVER
BIG CATS

Monalisa Sengupta

E **Enslow Publishers, Inc.**
40 Industrial Road
Box 398
Berkeley Heights, NJ 07922
USA

http://www.enslow.com

This edition published in 2009 by Enslow Publishers, Inc.

Original copyright © 2005 Really Useful Map Company (HK) Ltd.

Library of Congress Cataloging-in-Publication Data

Sengupta, Monalisa.
Discover big cats / Monalisa Sengupta.
p. cm. — (Discover animals)
Includes bibliographical references and index.
Summary: "Readers will learn how big cats hunt and live, where they
came from and why they are endangered"—Provided by publisher.
ISBN 978-0-7660-3473-0
1. Felidae—Juvenile literature. I. Title.
QL737.C23S46 2009
599.75—dc22

2008013725

Printed in China

10 9 8 7 6 5 4 3 2 1

To Our Readers: We have done our best to make sure all Internet Addresses in this book were active and appropriate when we went to press. However, the author and the publisher have no control over and assume no liability for the material available on those Internet sites or on other Web sites they may link to. Any comments or suggestions can be sent by e-mail to comments@enslow.com or to the address on the back cover.

Enslow Publishers, Inc., is committed to printing our books on recycled paper.
The paper in every book contains 10% to 30% post-consumer waste (PCW).
The cover board on the outside of each book contains 100% PCW.
Our goal is to do our part to help young people and the environment too!

Photo and Illustration Credits: Q2AMedia

Cover Photos and Illustrations: Q2AMedia

Contents

A Cat's World

Did you know that the common house cat is related to the lions and tigers that you may have seen at the zoo? They are members of the same family called *Felidae*. Each family is special and the curious world of cats is no different.

Meat lovers

Cats are hunters and love meat. Domestic cats hunt for mice, while lions, tigers and jaguars hunt in the wild. They prey on other wild animals for food.

■ The whole world is made up of what are called ecosystems, where living beings live interdependently and feed on one another. The big cats feed on smaller animals like deer, which eat grass and leaves. Such a cycle is called a food chain.

■ The king of the jungle is among the mightiest of all big cats.

INTERESTING FACT!

Cats have more bones than humans. Humans have only 206 bones in their body, whereas the cat has 230. About 10 percent of a cat's bones are in its tail. The tail is used to maintain balance.

Tail

On the prowl

They have large eyes, excellent hearing, sharp teeth and strong limbs with sharp claws. This makes them good hunters. Most have long tails and their fur is often spotted or striped.

■ Big cats have special hunting skills. Most like to stalk their prey before attacking.

FACT FILE

Number of species
36
Smallest cat
the rusty-spotted cat stands 7 inches (17 cm) tall and weighs less than 3 pounds (1.5 kg)
Biggest cat
tigers weigh as much as 714 pounds (324 kg) and can be as long as 14 feet (4.3 m)
Fastest cat
cheetahs can run as fast as 70 mph (130 km/h)
Average life span
15-20 years

Body structure

Most cats have similar skeletons. They have rounded heads and their body structure allows them to move swiftly and silently. Their backbone is very different from humans. While ours is very rigid, the cat's flexible spine allows it to bend into a ball!

Living den

Big cats are native to all continents except Australia and Antarctica. But most of the 36 species of wild cats are in danger. Some scientists believe that many of them may not be around within the next 20-40 years.

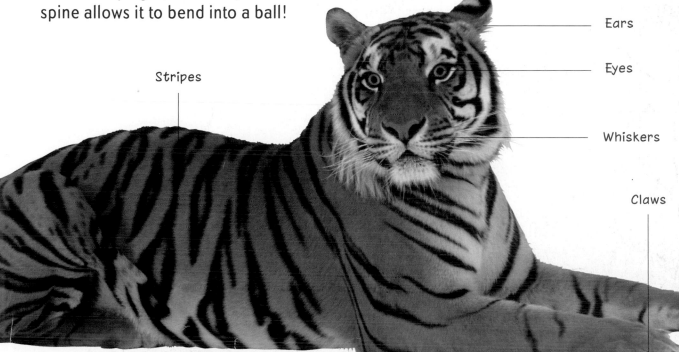

Stripes

Ears

Eyes

Whiskers

Claws

The First Cats

It is a common saying that a cat has nine lives. While that is not true, cats have been around for more than 30 million years. Modern cats evolved about 10-12 million years ago, and we are learning more about their evolution.

First cats

The earliest known cat is the Proailurus ("pro" means old and "ailurus" means cat), which lived about 30 million years ago. It was a small sized animal – the size of a small bobcat – and had a six-inch-long skull. This cat, which is extinct now, had more teeth than its modern cousins.

■ The Proailurus was a strong climber and spent most of its time in trees.

Toothy matter

Smilodon, a type of saber-toothed cat, had long, knife-like front teeth. It used its teeth to cut through its prey's skin, wounding it. The prey would then bleed to death. But the Smilodon's teeth were not strong enough to bite into bones and would sometimes break.

■ Saber-toothed cats had very powerful front legs and short tails. These cats were not fast runners but stalked their prey and attacked without warning.

Not tigers

The saber-toothed tiger is another prehistoric cat. Despite its name, it is not an ancestor of today's tigers. In fact, this big cat belonged to a separate branch of the cat family that became extinct millions of years ago.

FACT FILE
Weight of a Proailurus
20 pounds (9 kg)
Saber-tooth's canine size
8 inches (20 cm)
Smilodon was the size of
a modern African lion
Smilodon became extinct
about 10,000 years ago
Fossils of early cats
have been found in Africa, Europe, and North and South America

Tiger jaw

Common ancestor

Among modern cats, jaguars and leopards are believed to have had the same ancestor. But they moved to different areas over time and developed unique features. Lions, on the other hand, evolved more recently. They first lived in Western Africa nearly 750,000 years ago and then spread into Asia, Europe and America.

INTERESTING FACT!

The saber-toothed tiger probably lived on grassy plains and open woodlands, in and around North and South America. It lived in the last ice age, about 1.5 million years ago. It would have been a main predator at the time.

■ Early forms of the cheetah are believed to have inhabited North America as far back as 2.5 million years ago. Some scientists believe that cheetahs have ancestral links with the puma.

Cat Family

Cats in the wild are classified as small, medium and large depending on their size. They are also divided into three groups based on their traits. These are *Felinae*, *Pantherinae* and *Acinonychinae*.

Domestic vs wild

Domestic cats and their wild relatives share many characteristics. They have short, strong jaws and sharp teeth. All cats are good hunters. But while smaller cats like to eat standing, big cats like to lie down and eat their food.

■ Domestic cats hold their tails low and swing them to indicate that they are feeling playful or nervous. An upright tail is usually a sign of alertness. Big cats behave similarly.

■ The polecat has a long, slender body and short legs. It feeds on rats, mice, rabbits, fish, eggs and fruit but, despite its misleading name, it is not a member of the cat family. It is a type of weasel.

First pets

Archaeological studies show that human beings have kept pet cats for nearly 8,000 years. In Egypt, 4,000 years ago, they were kept because of their skill in hunting snakes, rats and mice. The Egyptians also worshipped cats and believed they were forms of the Goddess Bast. It was a crime to kill cats.

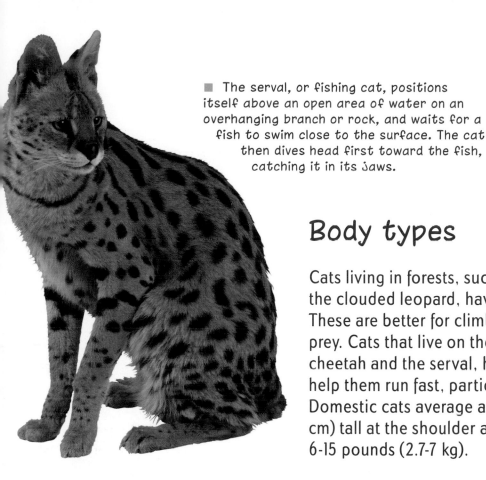

■ The serval, or fishing cat, positions itself above an open area of water on an overhanging branch or rock, and waits for a fish to swim close to the surface. The cat then dives head first toward the fish, catching it in its jaws.

Body types

Cats living in forests, such as the jaguar and the clouded leopard, have short, stocky limbs. These are better for climbing trees and ambushing prey. Cats that live on the savannah, such as the cheetah and the serval, have long limbs. These help them run fast, particularly when chasing prey. Domestic cats average about 8-10 inches (20-25 cm) tall at the shoulder and weigh from 6-15 pounds (2.7-7 kg).

Purr and meow

Some scientists say a domestic cat can make more than 60 different sounds and they may have different meanings. For example, a meow can be a friendly greeting, or it may express curiosity, hunger, or loneliness. Purring usually means contentment, but some cats also purr when they are sick. Hisses, growls, and screams indicate anger and fear.

INTERESTING FACT!

Despite its name, the polecat is actually a member of the weasel family and is related to the skunk and the ferret. Similarly, the Australian tiger cat is a marsupial that is closely related to the possum and the Tasmanian Devil.

■ Different types of cats can be cross-bred to give rise to new breeds, or hybrids. The liger, one of the most well-known hybrids, is obtained by interbreeding a lion and a tiger.

Cat Senses

These specialist hunters rely on their senses of sight and hearing to locate their prey. They also produce a wide range of sounds, including snarls, growls, purrs and roars. While lions and tigers roar, cheetahs and pumas tend to purr.

Looking afar

Big cats have excellent day and night vision. Their eyes face forward, allowing both eyes to focus on the same object. Their sharp eyesight allows them to judge distances and the size of the object as well.

■ Apart from its strong muscles and teeth, a tiger also relies on its senses for a successful hunt.

Vision at night

The big cat's eye is larger than a human's. A cat has a larger pupil, which allows more light to enter the eye at night. While a human pupil is always circular, the cat can shrink its pupil from a circle into a slit-like opening. It does so in bright sunlight, allowing less light to enter the eye.

INTERESTING FACT!

No one knows exactly how a cat sees color, but they definitely do not see it the way we do. According to most scientists, reds appear darker, while greens appear much lighter and duller to a cat.

■ A pair of glowing eyes can look scary at night.

Moving ears

Cats have very sharp hearing and can pinpoint the location of a sound almost immediately. The ear has nearly 20 muscles attached to it. The moment a cat hears a sound, it can move its ears in that direction.

Pinnae

■ The external ears of cats are shaped like cups and are called pinnae.

Marked territory

All cats have marked areas, or territories, where they live and will protect them fiercely from other cats. Territories usually include hunting grounds, dens, water spots and resting spots. Big cats mark these territories to warn other cats. They leave their scent by spraying urine in special locations or by scratching on trees. They can also leave their scent by rubbing their chins, cheeks, and tails onto objects.

■ Cats like tigers can smell the presence of another cat that has left its scent in a marked area.

Of Fur and Claws

Big cats are covered with fur. The fur coat protects the animal in very cold or hot weather. But, more importantly, the unique pattern on it acts as camouflage. Camouflage is the ability of an animal to blend with its surroundings. This makes them nearly invisible!

Tiger

Leopard

Cheetah

■ Cats have different patterns on their coats depending on the habitat in which they live.

Protective coat

Just as you wear wool sweaters in the winter, big cats living in cold areas have thick fur to protect them from the cold. The snow leopard has long, woolly fur which is longer on the animal's belly. This gives extra protection to the part of the body closest to the snow-covered ground. Cats living in warmer climates have short, bristly fur.

■ The small front teeth of the cat mainly function as grooming aids.

Invisible coat

A cat's coat is similar to its surroundings. The base color of the fur is similar to that of the habitat. The lion's yellow-brown fur matches the coloring of the savannah grasslands while stripes on the tiger's coat make it difficult to spot among the tall grasses. The spotted coat of the leopard mimics the patchy sunlight of the forest. Cubs often have spots that fade out as they grow.

■ With the exception of the cheetah, all cats have retractable claws. These claws stay inside the paws and come out only when in use, for example during combat.

Death grip

Claws are a very important hunting tool for cats. With the exception of the cheetah, all cat claws stay covered in their paws. This keeps them safe and sharp. Their claws help the big cats to climb trees, and are also handy while attacking prey or defending themselves.

INTERESTING FACT!
Long fur is not just to protect against the cold. The black-footed cat and sand cat both have longer fur covering their feet and pads. Both these cats live in desert areas, and the fur protects against the heat of the ground.

Grooming and more

The tongue of the wild cat is much rougher than that of the domestic cat. Its surface is covered with tiny hooks that helps the cat to clean and comb its fur. It also helps them to strip flesh off the bones of their prey.

■ An adult mountain lion may be either gray or reddish-yellow in color. It does not have any spots.

Young

Big cats, like human beings, give birth to their young. While a domestic cat's young are called kittens, a big cat's young are called cubs. The mother usually takes care of her cubs till they grow old enough to look after themselves. Cubs, like human babies, are quite helpless at birth. Some are even born blind!

Born weak

The mother moves her cubs from one hiding place to another to protect them. She carries them in her mouth, one at a time. Hyenas, leopards, and even other lions may kill cubs while the mother is away hunting.

Food habits

Cats are mammals, and for the first month and a half, the cubs live only on their mother's milk. When they are older, the mother leads them to an animal she has killed. Cats look after their young till they are about 18 to 24 months old – when they can hunt for themselves.

■ The lioness carries a cub in her mouth, holding it by the neck. Lion cubs have thick padding on their necks, which prevents the mother's teeth from injuring them.

■ Cubs depend on their mother's milk for about three to six months.

■ One-year-old cubs accompany their mothers on a hunt.

School time

The mother cat usually trains her cubs to hunt after their first year. She does this by bringing them live animals to catch and kill. The cub begins its training by copying the mother.

INTERESTING FACT!

Cubs chase each other and wrestle as they practice some of the skills they will need in their adult life. Sometimes the mother leads the prey to her cubs, so that they can practice their hunting skills.

■ Cheetahs hide their cubs in tree tops to protect them from predators.

Attack

The cat's body is perfectly built for hunting and killing. It has strong grasping limbs, sharp claws, and knife-like canine teeth. Most cats hunt at dawn or dusk and have excellent senses of vision and hearing. They often have patterned coats that help hide them from their prey.

■ The stripes on a tiger's body allow it to hide in the grass from its prey.

Run and pounce

When the cat senses the right moment, it transfers its body weight to its rear legs and lunges toward the victim. This begins the chase. If the cat gets close enough, the prey's run is short. The final phase is the pounce. The cat grabs the animal, and pulls it to the ground. Then it suffocates its prey with its mouth and kills it.

Stalk and ambush

Stalking is when the cat follows its prey silently before attacking. A hunting technique used when a cat hides and attacks suddenly is called an ambush. If an unsuspecting animal comes within striking distance, the cat comes out of hiding and lunges toward its surprised and unprepared victim.

■ The lioness is the main hunter in a group, although she is helped by her bigger cubs. The lion only joins in when the prey is big.

■ While cats approach very quietly, the prey is often alerted by other herd members. The entire herd then breaks into a run.

Special features for hunting

The snow leopard has a lot of power in its rear legs, making it capable of leaping 40 feet (12 m) along the ground. This is used to great effect in the final phase of hunting

The cheetah's special bone structure and muscles allow it to travel at speeds in excess of 70 mph (112 km/h) and it can 'out-chase' any animal

Final kill

Not all cats kill their prey in the same way. Small cats kill their prey with a bite to the back of the neck. Large cats suffocate their prey, either with a stranglehold on the neck or by covering the prey's snout with their jaws.

INTERESTING FACT!

Some cats like the caracal use their paws to catch birds. Just as the bird takes flight, the cat rises up on its hind legs, jumps up and catches its prey with an extended paw. Having caught the bird in both paws, it brings it down and eats it.

Success rate

The cheetah is the best hunter within the wild cat species. It catches up to 60-70 percent of prey that it hunts. The lion on the other hand has a low success rate at less than 30 percent.

■ Among the cheetah's hunting skills, the final chase down is its most effective weapon. A combination of physical features allow the cheetah to run faster than any other land animal.

Defense

While big cats are known to be the most deadly predators, many have had to develop methods to protect themselves from injury during a hunt. They also face threats from other cats who may take over their territory or try to steal their kill from them. Protecting the cubs is the responsibility of the female.

■ A leopard will climb a tree to protect its kill from other animals like lions and hyenas who have been known to steal their prey from them.

In the family

A lioness will protect her cubs from other animals and also from lions who pose a threat to them. When a new male lion takes over a pride, he usually kills all the cubs and mates with the lionesses to start his own family. The male lion protects the entire family. His mane makes him look larger to other lions.

■ A lioness defends the young ones in the pride. It will attack any wild animal that could harm her babies.

Group attack

Lions usually hunt together to increase their chances of killing prey and protecting themselves. They fan out in a semicircle to creep up on the prey. Lions have been known to be injured while hunting larger prey, like giraffes and elephants.

Defending territory

Big cats like tigers are very protective of their territory. One male's territory generally includes three to four females. Males will aggressively fight each other to defend their territory. However, neighboring females have been known to share their kill.

INTERESTING FACT!

Some cats attack in groups. A few cats act as "beaters," moving openly toward an intended victim and driving it in the direction of another cat lying in wait, ready to pounce. This strategy is used by both the lynx and the lion.

Animal attack

Other animals also have methods of defending themselves against the mighty cats. Elephants kick, rampage, trample and usually succeed in running away. Zebras snort loudly to alert the herd of impending danger. The males will position themselves between the predator and the herd and kick and bite, giving the herd time to escape. Animals like the wildebeest are known to break into a stampede.

■ When a herd of elephants face danger, the adults form a circle around the calves to protect them. Big cats, however, rarely attack elephants because of their sheer size.

King of the Savannahs

The lion is often called the king of beasts because it is so big and powerful and because it has no natural predators. The male lion has a mane around its neck that adds to its royal look. Its loud roar is fierce and frightening. Lions are truly majestic and exhibit dominant behavior.

Living in the open

Unlike tigers, lions don't like living in thick forests. They prefer to roam through open lands, and are usually found in woodlands, grassy plains, and areas with thorny scrub trees. Lions live where they find a steady supply of food, like deer, antelope, zebra and other hoofed animals. Lions also need to live near water.

In zoos and in the wild

Lions are found in eastern and southern Africa. A few hundred can be found in the Gir Forest of India. They are called Asiatic lions. Most lions live in national parks and areas called reserves, where the animals are protected from hunters. Hundreds of lions also live in zoos and are extremely popular performers in circuses.

Lion's mane

Lions are better known for their strength, rather than speed. Male lions are the only cats with manes. This collar of long, thick hair covers the head and the neck down to the shoulders and chest. The mane makes the male look bigger and stronger.

HABITAT

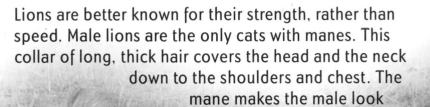

FACT FILE

Average weight
about 353-397 pounds (160-180 kg). A large male can weigh up to 507 pounds (230 kg)
Length
about 10 feet (3 m)
Height
about 3.2 feet (1 m) tall at the shoulder
Lioness weight
about 243-309 pounds (110-140 kg)
Lioness height
about 1 foot (30 cm) shorter than lions

INTERESTING FACT!

The lion's mane protects him during fights. The long, thick hair softens the enemy's blows. One-year-old cubs have little hair around their heads. The mane is not fully grown until the animal is about 5 years old.

■ Unlike most wild cats, who prefer to live alone, lions live in one big family, called a pride.

The cover of color

The lion's coat is ideal camouflage while hunting. It is a brownish yellow – the same color as dead grass. Only the back of the ears and the tuft of hair at the end of the tail are black. Cubs have spots on their coats.

■ The male lions in the pride ordinarily let the lionesses do the hunting for the family. But they kill for themselves when they find prey.

Living in Prides

Lions are the only big cats that live in a group, called a pride. A pride usually has 10 to 20 lions. A large pride may have as many as 35 lions. Each pride can have from one to five adult males, several lionesses, and cubs. Members of a pride stay together as a family. When they meet, they greet each other by rubbing cheeks.

■ While lions can climb trees if they have to, most of them avoid it. They are simply too heavy.

Marked area

Male cubs are usually chased from the territory by their fathers when they are between 2 and 3 years old. These young males then wander until they form their own pride. Each pride stays in a specific area called its territory. Lions do not allow strange predators to hunt in their territory.

Strong muscles

A lion's legs and shoulders are very muscular. They give the lion the strength to clutch its prey and pull it to the ground. Each paw has curved claws that hook and hold the prey. When not in use, each claw withdraws into the paw so the claws stay sharp.

■ Lions usually spend about 20 hours a day sleeping or resting. Hungry cubs nurse on any lioness that has milk and not just their own mothers.

Gulping food

Lions usually have 30 teeth. Four large pointed teeth are used to hold the prey, kill it, and to tear the meat. Four cheek teeth are used for cutting through the prey's tough skin and muscles. But the lion has no teeth for chewing. It swallows the food in chunks.

■ A lot of animals, like this African hunting dog and hyenas, feed on the leftovers that the lions leave behind.

INTERESTING FACT!

The Asiatic lion has a thicker coat and a more pronounced fringe of hair on its belly compared to the African lion. The tassel at the end of the Asiatic lion's tail is also considerably larger. However, its mane is much smaller.

■ Masai warriors are nomadic people, who live in Kenya. In the past, young men from the tribe had to kill a lion to prove that they were mature and strong. Today, this practice has been made illegal.

In danger

The Asiatic lion is an endangered species. African lions have a much better chance for survival. Africa has many reserves where lions may not be shot. The lion tries to avoid contact with people. It rarely attacks humans unless it is threatened, tormented or injured.

The Tiger Trail

The tiger is the largest member of the cat family. After the lion, tigers are perhaps the most awesome of all the big cats. In the old days, kings would hunt tigers for their beautiful fur. The large scale killing of tigers and clearing of forests have left just a few thousand of them in the wild today. Tigers live in the forests of Asia and are part of many a myth and story!

■ Tigers are extremely fast when running short distances and can leap nearly 30 feet (9 m). But if a tiger fails to catch its prey quickly, it will give up the moment it feels tired.

Striped giants

Tigers can be easily recognized because of their striped fur and skin. They usually have an orange or brownish yellow coat with a white chest and belly. Their coat is covered with broken vertical black or dark brown stripes. These stripes allow the animal to blend in while walking through tall grass.

Living in shadows

Tigers live in oak wood forests, tall grasslands, swamps and marshes. They are found in the hot rainforests of Malaya, the dry thorn woods of India and the cold, snowy spruce forests of northern China. Tigers rarely go into open spaces like lions do.

■ A tiger marks its territory with urine, claw marks, or by rubbing its tail against a tree or a rock. The scent and mark let other tigers know that the territory is occupied.

On the prowl

The tiger usually hunts at night, following animal trails along stream beds. A tiger uses its sharp eyes and keen ears for a hunt, along with its sense of smell. The tiger waits in cover, before rushing its prey and pouncing. Using its sharp claws, the tiger grasps its victim by the side and pulls it to the ground.

FACT FILE

Weight
423-714 pounds
(192-324 kg)
Length
9-11 feet (2.7-3.3 m)
Litter size
2 to 4 cubs
Cub weight
2-3 pounds (0.9-1.4 kg)
at birth
Life span
up to 20 years

■ Tigers are good swimmers and they enjoy wading in water, especially when it gets hot. Tigers can climb trees, but they do not usually do so because of their huge size.

Hearty meal

A tiger can go without food for a long time after a successful hunt. The tiger stays near the carcass until it has eaten everything except its bones and stomach. A tiger may eat over 88 pounds (40 kg) of meat in a night, gulping in the food rather than chewing it. A long drink and a nap often follow a meal.

■ Tigers prefer large prey, such as deer, antelope, wild oxen and wild pigs. Some tigers also attack elephant calves. Tigers especially like porcupines, but their quills cause them painful wounds.

INTERESTING FACT!

Adult tigers usually live alone, but they are not unsociable. Two tigers may meet on their nightly rounds. They rub heads together in a kind of greeting and then part ways. Tigers have also been known to share a kill as well.

Tigers in Danger!

There are eight sub-species of tiger. These are the Bali tiger, Bengal tiger, Caspian tiger, Indo-Chinese tiger, Javan tiger, Siberian tiger, South China tiger, and Sumatran tiger. Of these, the Bali tiger, Caspian tiger and Javan tiger are now extinct. The remaining five are also in danger of becoming extinct.

One family

The Indo-Chinese tiger is found in Thailand, south China, Myanmar, Cambodia, Vietnam and parts of Malaysia. These tigers are one of the smaller sub-species. The Siberian tiger is found in Russia and is the largest of all tiger species. The Sumatran tiger is only found on the Indonesian island of Sumatra. It is the smallest of all the tiger species. The South Chinese tiger is considered to be the evolutionary ancestor of all the other tiger sub-species. This tiger is the world's most endangered species.

■ The tigers of Siberia, where the winters are bitterly cold, have long, shaggy, winter coats.

Just a few

There are about 500 Siberian tigers in the wild and they are found mainly in Russia. The South China tiger is even rarer. Demand for tiger parts like the eyes, bones and skin for use in traditional Chinese medicine led to an increase in poaching after the 1980s. This has threatened the tiger with extinction.

Man eaters?

There are many tales about Great Bengal Tigers being ferocious man-eaters. Yet almost all wild tigers avoid people. Fatal attacks by tigers on humans are, thankfully, rare. Most tigers would only attack a human if disturbed, or were provoked or injured.

HABITAT

FACT FILE

Numbers in the wild
Great Bengal Tiger
3,030-4,735
Siberian Tiger
160-230
South China Tiger
20-50
Sumatran Tiger
400-500
Indo-Chinese Tiger
1,180-1,790

■ In the Sunderban Reserve, along the coast of the Bay of Bengal in India, tigers are reported to have attacked people. Since tigers are thought to attack only from the rear, the people there wear masks on the backs of their heads. This second "face" is thought to confuse the tigers and thus protect the wearer.

INTERESTING FACT!

Many adult males claim a territory as their own and keep other males out. The territory may average about 20 square miles (52 sq km) and usually includes a body of water. Tigers also communicate by using different sounds.

White Bengal tigers

Some tigers have chalk-white fur with chocolate-brown or black stripes. These tigers are called white tigers and they have blue eyes. All other tigers have yellow eyes. White tigers are very rare in the wild. More than 100 white tigers live in the world's zoos.

■ White tigers are a variant of Bengal tigers and are rarely found in the wild anymore. A normal-colored female can give birth to a litter in which some of the cubs are white.

Leopards

Leopards are the third largest big cats, after tigers and lions. They are excellent climbers and, unlike most other wild cats, love living in trees. These cats can in live in various kinds of habitats and also have a wide range of prey. They live in the Saharan regions of Africa, and many Asian countries like Turkey, Korea, Java, India and China.

Leopards spend most of their lives on tree tops.

Clear markings

The leopard is most easily recognized by its rosette patterned coat and extremely long tail which is darker than the rest of its body. The base color of the coat varies according to the leopard's habitat. Leopards living in open grasslands are golden yellow, while those found in deserts are yellow or cream in color. Leopards living in mountain regions are deep gold in color.

Night hunter

Leopards usually hunt at night, though females with cubs prefer to hunt during the day. These cats hunt all kinds of prey, be it impalas, gazelles, hares, reptiles, small monkeys, or various rodents such as rats, squirrels and porcupines.

Clouded leopards have cloud-like spots on their skin. Found in southeastern Asia, they often hang upside down from tree branches!

HABITAT

FACT FILE

Can grow as long as
8 feet (2.5 m)
Can be as tall as
2 feet (70 cm)
Average weight
66-198 pounds
(30-90 kg)
Litter Size
1-4 on average
Life Span
12-17 years

■ Snow leopards, found in the snow-capped mountains of Russia, China and the Himalayas, have woolly fur. Interestingly, their voices are weak and they cannot roar like other big cats.

Strong and mean

Leopards have very strong muscles and can drag a fully grown male antelope or even a young giraffe—weighing up to three times their own body weight—high into the tree tops. Leopards are also known to attack humans and their livestock and can be more dangerous than tigers or lions.

Killed for fur

But humans have also been a threat to these cats. They have killed leopards for their fur. As a result leopards have become rare in many places. Many countries have banned trade in leopard skins to protect the animal.

INTERESTING FACT!

All black leopards - sometimes called black panthers - are found in the dense, wet forested areas of India and Southeast Asia. Their dark color gives them an advantage while hunting.

■ Vervet monkeys make a loud barking call when a leopard is near to alert the rest of their group.

The Swiftest

The fastest animal on earth, the cheetah is unique in many ways. It looks like a large muscular greyhound, with a sleek body and long, thin, but powerful legs. This gives the big cat great speed while on the chase. A fully-grown cheetah can reach speeds greater than 70 mph (113 km/h)!

■ Cheetahs live in dry areas like bush lands, savannah and semi-deserts and feed on gazelles, impala, wildebeest and zebra.

Following prey

The cheetah hunts mainly by day. It first follows a large herd of gazelle, impala or antelope from a distance. It then selects old, injured or young animals as its prey. The cheetah then chases the animal. The cheetah usually catches its prey in the first attempt.

The kill

The cheetah's powerful jaw muscles enable the cat to grip its prey for several minutes and suffocate the animal by clamping the windpipe. The cheetah has enlarged nasal passages, which enables it to breathe more easily while on the run.

■ Once the kill has been made the cheetah rests to regain its breath. At this time it is vulnerable to hyenas snatching its kill.

■ The cheetah's paws are like a dog's. They are narrow with hard pads and non-retractable claws, unlike other big cats. This allows better grip while running.

HABITAT

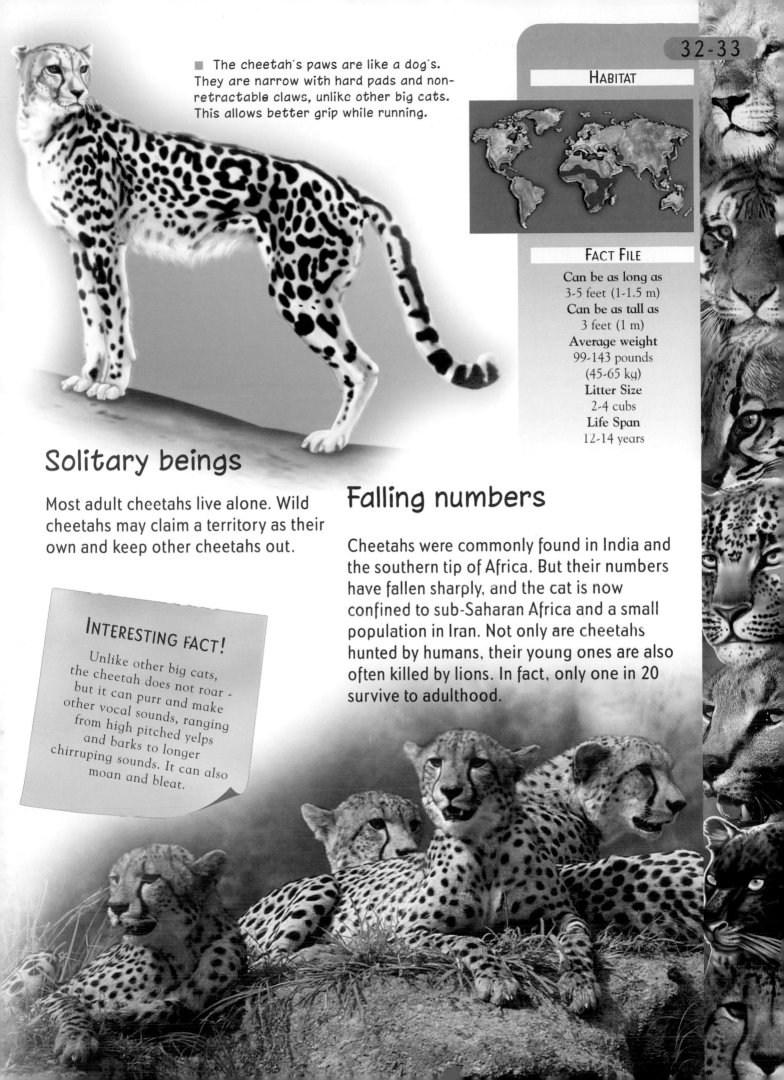

FACT FILE

Can be as long as
3-5 feet (1-1.5 m)
Can be as tall as
3 feet (1 m)
Average weight
99-143 pounds
(45-65 kg)
Litter Size
2-4 cubs
Life Span
12-14 years

Solitary beings

Most adult cheetahs live alone. Wild cheetahs may claim a territory as their own and keep other cheetahs out.

INTERESTING FACT!

Unlike other big cats, the cheetah does not roar - but it can purr and make other vocal sounds, ranging from high pitched yelps and barks to longer chirruping sounds. It can also moan and bleat.

Falling numbers

Cheetahs were commonly found in India and the southern tip of Africa. But their numbers have fallen sharply, and the cat is now confined to sub-Saharan Africa and a small population in Iran. Not only are cheetahs hunted by humans, their young ones are also often killed by lions. In fact, only one in 20 survive to adulthood.

Jaguars of America

Jaguars are often confused with leopards. Both have a similar brownish-yellow base fur color, with dark rosette markings. But jaguars can be identified by the small dots or irregular shapes within the larger rosette markings. They are more stocky and muscular and have a shorter tail.

Living zone

The jaguar is the biggest cat found in the Americas. Jaguars once inhabited areas between the southern states of the U.S. down to the tip of South America. But their population is now mostly limited to the north and central parts of South America. These big cats prefer to live in forest areas, though they have been spotted around dry woodland and grasslands.

■ Black jaguars are often wrongly called black panthers or black leopards. But a good way to identify them is by their large head and stocky forelimbs.

Great variety

The body of a jaguar often depends on its habitat. Those living in dense forested areas are smaller than the ones living in open areas. Forest dwellers are also darker in color for better camouflage.

■ Females keep their cubs safe in caves, rocky dens or holes in the forest floor.

■ Jaguars climb trees, though they are not as agile as leopards. These cats prefer to hunt monkeys in the lower branches of trees of the rainforest.

HABITAT

FACT FILE

Length
5-8 feet (1.5-2.5 m)
Average weight
154-265 pounds
(70-120 kg)
Litter Size
1-4 cubs
Life Span
12-16 years
Size of cub
1.5-2 pounds
(0.7-1 kg)

In danger

There was a sharp fall in the jaguar population in the 1960s and 1970s. As many as 18,000 jaguars were killed every year for their coats. While jaguar fur is no longer in fashion, the big cat is still under threat. Many organizations are trying to protect the animal and the forests where they live.

INTERESTING FACT!

Jaguars are revered in many ancient cultures. The Mayans believed that Jaguar, the god of the underworld, helped the sun to travel under the Earth at night, making sure that it rose again the following morning.

Munching time

Even its hunting habits vary according to its habitat. If they live close to humans, jaguars hunt at night. Jaguars that live in the wild prefer to hunt during the day. They hunt cattle, horses, deer, reptiles, monkeys and even fish.

■ Jaguars like to live close to water. They are experts in catching fish and will often tackle turtles, dragging them out from the water and crushing their shells with their powerful jaws.

Lynx and Ocelot

Not all big cats are as huge as lions, tigers or leopards. Lynx and ocelots are much smaller in size but that does not make them any less awesome. Both these animals are good hunters. But, like most big cats, they too are in danger of extinction.

Hungry lynx

Lynx live in parts of Africa, Asia, Europe, and North America. They prefer to stay in forests or in rocky, brush-covered places. They hunt mainly at night and feed on rabbits and other small animals. A hungry lynx can even kill fox and deer.

Spots and stripes

The lynx's fur grows long all over its body. The fur is light gray or grayish-brown, long and silky. It is spotted and striped with a darker shade. Lynx have stubby tails and long tufts of hair on their pointed ears.

■ The lynx has huge feet with thick fur cover. These act as snowshoes and help it run swiftly over snow in winter. Lynx sleep in caves or hollow trees. They like to climb trees and lie on the branches.

Dots galore

The ocelot's fur color varies from reddish-yellow to smoky-pearl in color. Its body is covered with black spots of different sizes. The spots on its legs and feet are like dots, while other body parts can have shell-shaped spots. The ocelot has a pink nose and large, translucent eyes.

■ Although similar in appearance to the lynx, the bobcat has relatively shorter legs and smaller paws.

Meal time

The ocelot is also known as the leopard cat or tiger cat of the U.S. The ocelot lives in an area ranging from Texas to northern Argentina. It eats mice, wood rats, rabbits, snakes, lizards, birds, young deer and monkeys.

■ Ocelots are widely hunted for their fur and their numbers have decreased sharply. There are now laws to stop the killing of ocelots.

Pumas

A cat of many names, the puma is also known as the cougar, panther or mountain lion. It is found in Canada, North America and parts of South America. The puma has a small, broad head with small rounded ears. The cat's body is powerful, with long hind legs and a tail with a black tip.

■ Pumas have between one and five cubs at a time, generally two years apart. The average number is three.

Coats of many colors

An adult puma may be either gray or reddish-yellow in color. Its fur is fawn-gray tipped with reddish-brown or grayish color. This animal has no spots, which is one of the main differences between a puma and a jaguar. They can also be solid black in color.

Hunting skills

While on the hunt, the puma uses the strength of its powerful back legs to lunge at its prey with a single jump while it is still running. A puma can pounce over 40 feet (12 m).

■ A puma keeps under cover while stalking its prey. It then pounces, breaking its prey's neck or dragging it down to the ground.

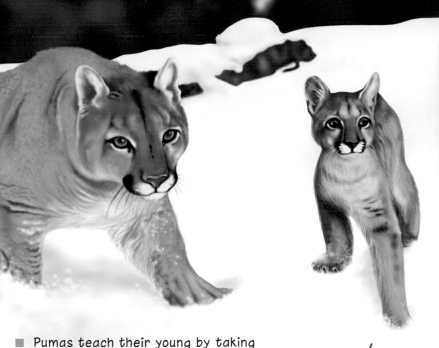

HABITAT

FACT FILE

Average length
more than 5 feet (1.5 m)
Can be as heavy as
227 pounds (103 kg)
The male is 1.4 times
the size of the female
Life span
10 to 20 years
Cubs weigh
1 pound (0.5 kg)
at birth

■ Pumas teach their young by taking them on hunts. The cub observes how the mother stalks and finally kills the prey.

Variety of food

The puma hunts alone by day or night and will hide its food in dense undergrowth, returning to it over several days. Large prey like elk may provide food for over a week. The puma can tackle larger prey such as domestic cattle or horses. The killing of livestock is one the main reasons that man hunts the puma. Puma also hunt wild deer, sheep, rodents, rabbits, hare, porcupines, squirrels, insects, fish and beavers.

INTERESTING FACT!

The cry of the mountain lion can be very scary. Unlike the deep roar of the African or Asiatic lion, it is shrill and sounds like a human being screaming. The puma can also roar softly. This sounds like a soft whistle.

Numbers dropping

Widespread hunting and trapping by humans has led to a drop in the number of pumas in the wild. The Florida panther, a kind of puma, is in great danger. Only 80 to 100 of these pumas are living in the wild today. Pumas shy away from human beings and are unlikely to attack them.

Closest Relatives

Big cats are not the only predators roaming the jungles. These cats have many close relatives like the hyena and civet. These animals might not look like cats, but they are, in fact, close relatives of cats.

Cat-like looks

The civet is a furry animal that looks somewhat like a long, slender cat. But a civet has a more pointed snout, a fluffier tail, and shorter legs than a cat. Their fur may be black, brown, gray, or tan and can even have dark spots. Civets live in Asia and in Africa. They feed on mice, rats, chickens and raid fruit orchards.

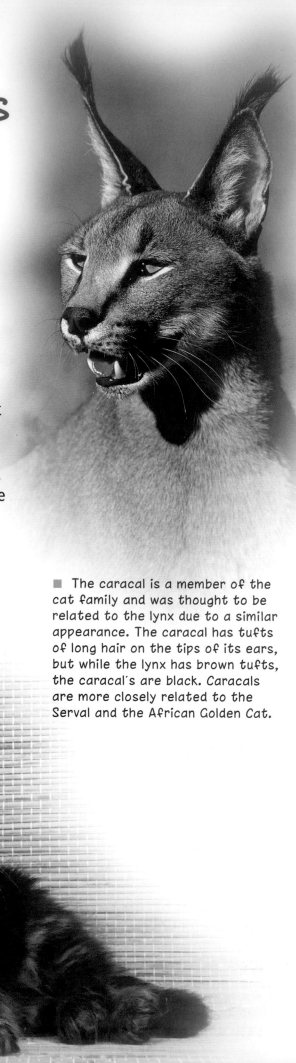

■ The cat family is made up of many different kinds of animals. But from the domestic cat to those in the wild, all are related.

■ The caracal is a member of the cat family and was thought to be related to the lynx due to a similar appearance. The caracal has tufts of long hair on the tips of its ears, but while the lynx has brown tufts, the caracal's are black. Caracals are more closely related to the Serval and the African Golden Cat.

Not a dog!!

Although they look more like dogs, hyenas are actually closer related to the cat family. Hyenas can be spotted, striped or brown in color. They hunt animals like zebras, gazelles, and buffalo for food. They also eat the remains of animals they find dead. Some species will steal the kills of other, larger cats.

■ The spotted hyena has a very scary cry. It sounds like loud hysterical laughter. These animals are often called laughing hyenas.

Living in clans

Like lions, hyenas also live in groups, or clans. These clans have a strict hierarchy in which the females dominate, followed by the cubs, with the males at the bottom. The most dominant in the hierarchy gets the best share of food and care. Young hyenas are very aggressive and twins begin to fight immediately after birth. Unlike other cubs, hyenas are strong at birth with open eyes and sharp canines. This can result in fighting cubs sometimes killing each other.

Similar sounding

Meerkats are not actually cats as their name suggests, but they are closely related. The meerkat is a type of mongoose found in African grasslands. It is a good hunter and eats bugs, lizards and small rodents. Unlike most mongooses, meerkats live in large groups.

■ Meerkats live in burrows and tunnels made in the ground. Meerkats watch out for each other, and are often seen on their hind feet with their noses in the air, looking around.

Endangered Cats

Though big cats are powerful and strong animals, their survival is threatened today. Over the past century, there has been a sharp fall in their numbers. Many types of these beautiful animals have become endangered, which has led to the formation of many organizations dedicated to their protection.

Loss of territory

The biggest threat to cats is the loss of their natural homes. As humans continue to cut down forests and clear grasslands, these animals are left with very few places to live. To make matters worse, humans also hunt these animals, leading to a further loss of lives.

Priceless parts

Hunting big cats was a favorite sport for many kings and lords in the past. These animals are also hunted for their skin, fur and body parts. These items often sell for a high price on the black market.

■ In the last 100 years the tiger population has fallen by half. There are very few tigers left on the planet.

■ In China and Far East Asia, organs and bones of tigers and leopards are used in special medicinal potions.

INTERESTING FACT!

The clouded leopard is hunted for its skin and its teeth. In Asian markets, these are sold as decorations, while the bones are used to make medicines. Some restaurants in Thailand and China serve cooked leopard meat.

Protection

Many organizations have taken steps to protect the big cats. Special areas or reserves have been made for these animals where they can be safe. Zoos are developing ways to make sure the cats have more babies. Many countries have also put a stop to the sale of fur and body parts from most endangered wild cats.

Project Tiger

One of the largest projects started to protect big cats is Project Tiger. It began in the 1970s in India. The project led to the opening of nine tiger reserves, which soon increased to 20. These reserves provide the tigers with a safer place to live.

Glossary

Ambush: Hiding and waiting to attack by surprise

Ancestor: An older member of a family, usually deceased

Camouflage: The ability to hide or blend in with one's surroundings

Carcass: The body of a dead animal

Domestic: Living near or in human habitation; animals that are accustomed to living with or near humans

Ecosystem: An area in which different animals and plants exist interdependently within the same environment

Endangered: Those species that are in danger of becoming extinct

Evolution: The process by which the traits of a species change over a long period of time, as individuals with the traits best suited to their environment survive and reproduce

Extinct: A species that has been wiped out of existence

Felidae: The family to which all cats belong. The name feline comes from this word

Food chain: The system in which larger animals feed on weaker animals and organisms

Grooming: To clean and make neat

Habitat: The place where an animal or plant naturally lives

Hybrid: A mix of two animals or plants of different species

Litter: A group of cubs born to the same mother at the same time

Lunge: To suddenly jump forward or run toward

Marsupial: Mammals in which the females carry their young in a pouch

Predators: Animals that prey on other animals for food

Prehistoric: That part of history for which no written record is available

Prey: An animal that is hunted by another animal for food

Pupil: The small opening in the eye that lets in light

Retractable: Something that can be pulled back

Rosette: A marking that looks like a rose

Saharan regions: The desert regions of North Africa

Savannah: The grasslands of Africa. In North America they are called the prairies and in South America they are called the pampas

Species: A group of animals or plants that have similar characteristics and can reproduce together

Spruce forests: A forest made up of a kind of evergreen pine tree

Stalk: To chase prey silently

Stealth: To do something secretly or quietly

Tissue: A group of cells in any living being

Further Reading

Books

Frisch, Aaron. *Lions.* Mankato, MN: Creative Education, 2007.

Hirschi, Ron. *Lions, Tigers, and Bears: Why Are Big Predators So Rare?* Honesdale, PA: Boyds Mills Press, 2007.

Huggins-Cooper, Lynn. *Big Cats.* North Mankato, Minn: Smart Apple Media, 2006.

Internet Addresses

Big Cat Rescue
http://www.bigcatrescue.org/index.htm

Cheetahspot.com
http://www.cheetahspot.com

World Wildlife Fund Species Finder
http://www.worldwildlife.org/species/index.html

Index